Inspirations

21 Daily Reflections for Rediscovering Your Authentic Self

By:
Stephanie Clark, PMHNP
Psychiatric/Mental Health Nurse Practitioner

Cover photo credit: Brandon Clark
Cover design and formatting: www.caligraphics.net

TABLE OF CONTENTS

Foreword

Life can be a long and complicated journey. Each life is different with distinct challenges. Yet, even with the uniqueness of every individual, there are common questions that we all must face. "Am I worthy of love?" "Does my life matter?" "What is my purpose?" These are powerful questions that impact us all and direct our lives.

The fear of not being worthy or good enough appeared for me in my own life in a variety of ways. As a mental health provider, I could see that many of the people I worked with struggled with similar issues also. I began to look inside myself and reflect on my own fears, digging into my own inner knowing to find answers that could provide me comfort. This book is the end product of that personal journey.

I wrote the following stories originally for myself. They were born from images or messages I would receive in meditation practice. I started to share these stories with others, who also felt inspired by them. With much love and encouragement, I have put these stories together in the book you are now reading with the hope that others will start to see themselves in a different way, as I now do.

The following daily exercises are meant to address the deep-rooted issues that live inside of us all. The stories and reflections are messages of hope and love. They are universal messages that speak to the human condition. They are not intended to preach a certain doctrine but are meant to inspire, promote, and spread a message of acceptance and validation regardless of who is reading them.

The term "Spirit" in these works refers to the ever-present Life Source that exists all around us. It is a term that I feel fits this energy best, as it uplifts my own spirit and is present in all things. However, if there is a term that feels better to you or a term that you feel more comfortable using for your own beliefs, change it out so that the following speaks to you in the truest sense.

These stories have a message that is both simple and profound, specific, and expansive. Some may impact you more than others. Many have the same message in different forms or speak to the same issues. This is intentional, as revisiting the same topic in a variety of ways helps to solidify the message.

I have designed this book to be a 21-day experience in rejecting fear and embracing love. You are welcome to read all the reflections at once, but I feel the messages are best understood as stand-alone daily exercises. I would encourage you to read one a day, then review the reflection questions at the end of the story and try out the mantra in your daily life if it resonates with you.

My hope for you after reading *Inspirations* is that you will begin to think of yourself as someone who is worthy of love and deserves an abundant existence. I know these messages have helped me to feel empowered in my own life.

When I was journaling about being anxious to share this work with others, I received the message of "Inspirations is an outward manifestation of your inner consciousness and what can be greater?" May this speak to you in a way that allows you to shine like never before.

Exercise 1: Forgiveness

Scissors

No one in this life is perfect. You will make mistakes in your lifetime, as will others. Sometimes other people are unkind, disrespectful, and cause you pain. This can be intentional or unintentional on their part. Sometimes people are so far removed from their own spirit and sense of humanity that they are unable to access the truest part of themselves, which is pure love. This results in a life being driven by the ego and fear, which can produce painful outcomes.

Other times you feel hurt by someone when no hurt was intended. This is usually due to past conditioning on your part. Another person's comment or action triggers a deep-seated wound, and you experience the pain all over again. There are times that you likely have inflicted similar pain to others, even if you were not aware of it, as you cannot know the history that every person carries. Being hurt by others is a situation that we all will face. At times, this is out of your control and is unprovoked. You may end up harboring resentment or ill will towards other people who have inflicted pain on you. You may see yourself as the victim and feel that you are justified in your resentment and judgments of them.

Many hold a belief that to forgive someone is "weak," or that by forgiving another, you are excusing their past poor behavior. This is a false perception. The truth is that forgiveness neither excuses other's behavior nor makes you become somehow weakened. Forgiveness has the opposite effect and is fortifying.

You cannot change other people. It is impossible to walk their path and alter how they treat you. You cannot force someone to feel sorry for what they have done or said. You cannot force someone to see your exact perspective, as no one sees your life exactly as you do.

The only thing you are in charge of is your own behavior and your own energy. You are in control of the way you think of yourself and others. You are in control of the resentful feelings you harbor against others, be they justified or not. You are in control of having judgmental and negative thoughts. These negative emotions are steeped in fear and weigh down your day-to-day existence.

As you walk your path, remember that each time someone mistreats you that you face a choice. The event occurs, someone has caused you pain. Someone has placed a heavy stone in your path. You have two options, acknowledge this obstacle and move around it, or lift the stone and strap it to your back. You may wonder why would anyone strap a heavy stone to their back and carry this burden with them. To look at the situation from this perspective, it would seem strange to choose to weigh yourself down with an unwanted load. However, every time you elect to harbor resentment and judgments against others, this is exactly the choice that you are deciding on.

As life unfolds and you encounter unpleasant situations, you may choose time and time again to lift up the stones, strap them to your back with rope, then continue to trudge along. To live this way is exhausting and painful, both physically and emotionally. The stones weigh your body down and begin to slowly break your back. Emotionally, the stones create an energy of heaviness, and your mind grows weary. A person living this way moves along their path slowly, as each stone impedes their progress. Even if a person can sense their life's purpose and what work needs to be finished, it is hard to advance with years of stones crushing your daily existence.

To become aware of your burdens is the first step. For many, they have carried the stones for so long that they do not even remember that this is not the natural way that a body should feel. They can no longer feel the stones as separate. The stones feel like a part of their actual physical existence. Once you become aware of the stones' presence, try to identify them. See the stones for what they really are, an outside experience that happened to you that you then chose to carry from that moment forward.

The second step is to look down at your hands. You have been carrying scissors with you this entire time. The scissors are made of forgiveness. Allow the scissors to free you from your heavy load. Cut away the cords and feel the difference in your body and spirit. You are slowly freeing yourself from the colossal weight of judgments and resentments. Let the stones fall and leave them where they land on the path. You are free of them now.

Notice how the stones did not disappear. You did not erase or excuse the past by cutting the stones from your back. You simply are giving yourself the gift of being able to walk upright for the first time in so long, stretching your weary back and looking upward to the sky. You are giving yourself the gift to move forward on your path, vivacious and light.

You could decide to go back and sit on the stones, kick them around, or be stuck again, but why move backward? This is not progress. Acknowledge the past painful memories and accept that you chose to strap the stones to yourself. Decide to forgive yourself for this and release the past. Allow it to stay on the ground. Feel the relief, and keep your eyes ever looking forward, not back. Know that there will be more stones ahead, as no path is totally free of obstacles. Remember that you, again, have a choice to move past the stones or strap them onto you once more. Sometimes it takes practice to remember that all stones can remain on the ground.

Your scissors are always sharp and ready. Forgiveness is a tool that is always available for you to use. It is easy to carry, as it weighs nothing. Keep your scissors in your hand and move forward knowing that you have the ability and capacity to overcome any obstacle. No stone is so enormous that you are forced to remain stuck behind it forever. No stone has the requirement that you must pick it up.

Also, remember that you can use your scissors to cut the cords of the stones that you have created for yourself. Your own self-judgments and guilt for past mistakes all become stones that you carry with you. You are worthy of releasing yourself from carrying these burdens. You are worthy of forgiveness, as all souls are.

Use your scissors daily. Love and forgive yourself. Love and forgive others. The stones in your life are the same stones that many struggle with.

It is impossible to cut another's binding cords for them, but you can show others the tools that you carry that have allowed you to be free. Encourage others to look down at their capable hands. Set an example to others by walking upright and unimpeded. Appreciate how light you feel with the beautiful energy of forgiveness always surrounding you, stretching your glorious body upright to the sky.

Reflection Questions/Exercises:

1. What are the burdens, or resentments that you are choosing to carry for yourself? How does this impact your daily existence? Are there any resentments that you are willing to release at this time? Is there a particular burden that is the most wearisome?

2. For today, sit in a quiet, meditative state for 10-15 minutes. You may want to set a timer to go off at the allotted time, or you may choose to just do the meditation experience until it feels right for you to stop. To start, sit in a comfortable position and try to limit interruptions. Close your eyes and start to take slow, deep breaths. Focus on your breathing, inhaling and exhaling. Next, imagine yourself releasing one of your stones, one resentment that you are willing to let go of, to the ground. Visualize yourself cutting this past hurt/resentment away. Feel the stone leave your body and land on the ground. See the stone as detached and separate from you. Now sit for the remainder of the meditation time with the sensation of you being free of this burden. During your meditation experience, if you find yourself getting distracted, focus back on your breathing until you feel centered again, and then continue with your exercise. Journal afterward about any emotions or resistance that came up for you during this experience.

Daily Mantra:

"I cut away the stones of resentment and give myself the gift of forgiveness."

Exercise 2: Releasing Limitations

Necklaces

Everyone is born with personal power. You know as a child that you have the capacity and potential to be anything, to do anything. You are not born with a belief that your possibilities are limited. This infinite potential is like an endless string of beads. You have the power to make any design, any necklace of your choosing. You are born with this glowing, beaded ring of possibilities surrounding you, and you are free to choose any belief for yourself. However, as you grow and learn from the environment, you start to absorb limiting views that you incorporate into a working image of yourself. You believe what others are telling you and start to forget the fullness of your potential as you see yourself as restricted. This is like giving away the beads on your necklace, one piece at a time. If you start to believe that there are options that are not open to you or that you are not good enough, the beads that you feel you have to choose from start to diminish.

Beads—or beliefs—on your necklace, can be transient or long-lasting. There are some beliefs you only wear for a time, and some you may wear for a lifetime. Some beads are life affirming and look brilliant and shiny. Other beads are wearisome and dull, like beliefs you hold about yourself that are self-limiting or self-defeating. Some beads clash with others and are always at odds with each other. Some you despise but wear out of honor or duty. You may be unsure of yourself and ask other people which beads, or beliefs, you should wear. Allowing others to choose your beads drains you of your personal power. Giving away this power starts to feel like you are wearing chains around your throat, slowly choking you until you are barely able to breathe. It could start to seem hopeless, as these inauthentic beliefs that are limiting your life make your necklace seem stifling. There is a bigger part of you that can feel the heaviness in your body that these beads produce and wonders if there is another way.

Know that there is an alternative route that you could take. Remember the important fact that you are the designer of the necklace and all necklaces are changeable. You are not doomed to any particular design or string of beads. You are not required to hold any beliefs about yourself that do not enhance your life. Give yourself permission to remove your necklace and take a close look at the beads that surround you each day. What beliefs are limiting you? You may be surprised to see that the beads that you have worn for many years are weighing you down. For example, are you sick of wearing perfectionism? It is a heavy bead that is never accepting of any other beads, no matter how you arrange them. Remove it and throw it away. Release yourself from feeling that this bead represents you. Choose beads that affirm your worth and remind you that you are a being of infinite potential. Work on rearranging or changing the beads until your beliefs about yourself no longer feels like a noose, but a collection of diamonds that surrounds you and shines luminously.

Lastly, believe that you are worthy of wearing this string of diamonds. You are worthy of only holding beliefs about yourself that are loving and supportive. Let the feeling of the strong stones protect you like armor. Any potential is open to you when your necklace is not a burden, but a support to hold your head high. Believe in your potential and worthiness so strongly that no one is able to steal this circle of radiant truth from you. If you allow it, these beliefs will shine brightly for you until the end of this life, never becoming dull, but forever glowing authentically.

Reflection Questions/Exercises:

1. Which beads are you currently wearing on your necklace? What beliefs about yourself do you carry around daily? What kind of thoughts do you have about your own capabilities and worth? Are these beliefs burdensome or supportive?

2. In your journal, draw the necklace that you currently are wearing. Honestly take a look at the beliefs that you carry around with you regarding yourself. There is likely a mix of positive and negative perceptions. Some examples of limiting beliefs may be, "I am not lovable," "I am not good enough," or "I am stupid." Now on another page, draw a new necklace, only selecting beads/beliefs that are life affirming and supportive. These could be beliefs such as, "I am capable," "I am worthy," "I am loved," or "I am smart." Look at your new belief necklace that you have just designed and focus on how it would feel to believe all these positive things about yourself. Imagine yourself putting this necklace around your neck, and work on incorporating these positive beliefs into your self-image. Look at the picture of your new belief chain then look in the mirror and practice saying the positive beliefs aloud. The more you affirm your positive beliefs to yourself, the more you will start to embrace them.

Daily Mantra:
   "I am the creator of my own necklace."

Exercise 3: Mindfulness

Coins

In each moment, Spirit is offering up coins of opportunities and wonder. These coins are presented as now moments—life experiences—which can be exciting, mundane, painful, or joyous. There is a constant stream of coins that are available to you, as life is a series of now moments, always in motion.

These life moments, or coins, will bring up emotions in you based on your past experiences and current perceptions you hold about yourself and others. As such, some coins can be painful to experience, which makes it challenging to be in the present moment. Coins can start to feel like burdens when they bring up unpleasant emotions. Daily tasks can become mundane, which makes it easy to "check out" and not be aware of your surroundings. Some people may feel that it is easier to power through their life on overdrive. Collecting the coins thoughtlessly, having thousands of small daily experiences, yet never living even one of them.

Others may feel that they are too busy to stop and appreciate the now moment. They may not even be aware of the coins around them. Society promotes a fast-paced existence, which encourages you to do as much as possible in a day. There are many demands that must be met, many "to do's" to check off. This is a future-focused way of thinking, where the current moment is seen as just a stepping-stone for something greater in the future. This is the same as someone who quickly grabs their coins, hoarding them away without a second glance, thinking that they will spend the coins in the future when it is the "right time." The truth is that you can waste your life, "collecting" moments—knowledge and opportunities—not living them fully, but waiting to trade them in for something better. Stashing them all away for a time in the future that you feel is somehow better than the current moment.

Yet, opportunities pass. The present moment is fleeting and cannot be collected to be cashed in later. It is an illusion that you are guaranteed time in the future to spend your coins. It is an illusion that coins gain value the longer you store them. You only have the true value of the coin at this moment. As time passes, coins lose their luster or dissipate. A seemingly full purse of past experiences, never fully lived, but hastily snatched up and saved only turns into regret and empty space. The fact is that you leave the bag behind when you depart from this life. Your inner spirit will pass on, and the only remaining thing will be a bag sitting on the ground, full of dull coins, missed opportunities that have turned to dust.

Coins are not meant to be saved. There is no assigned value to this moment versus the next. Each moment is priceless and gone in a fleeting glance. It is only your attention that seemingly adds more value to one moment compared to the next, as you see the current moment through a lens of past conditioning and judge it accordingly. Experiences and daily moments are gifts from Spirit. Every moment has value and is relevant to your life now. No experience is random or a mistake.

Cash in the coins moment to moment. Be present in your current life. Notice the coins Spirit is presenting to you. They are meant to be an investment into your current life, not an investment for the future. The value of the coins are always the highest at this moment. Fill up in each moment with the richness and depth of your surroundings. Revel in the joyful moments. Appreciate the small and great wonders of your life. Have the courage to be fully present even in difficult times. There is a reason that you are experiencing this situation, even if it is painful. Ignoring the challenging coins—or hiding them away—will only assure that you will encounter that difficult coin again in the future, as your life lessons will continue to appear until you have fully addressed them.

Work on becoming present in your daily life by mindfulness or meditation. Take an honest look at how you choose to distract yourself and set an intention to reduce these distractions. Observe how it feels to stay in the present moment versus living only in your mind. An easy place to start is to stay connected to your breathing. When your mind starts to spin or gets caught up in a chaotic spiral, pause and take a moment to breathe. Whatever you are doing, stop and take ten deep breaths in and out. Instead of thinking about your current situation, just breathe and allow yourself to simply be in your current situation. Now from this more grounded place, reconnect to the experience happening around you—the present moment—and act accordingly.

It can be difficult to stay present. However, it is the most meaningful thing you can do for yourself, to start to be an active participant in your life, versus a passive observer. Being present is the surest way to notice the gifts—the coins—that are all around you. There are so many coins from Spirit that are waiting to be noticed. The hope is that at the end of your life, you will leave a trail of coins, each one having been spent moment to moment, appreciating the life you have lived and knowing that Spirit invested in you every day you were alive.

<u>Reflection Questions/Exercises:</u>

1. In what ways do you distract yourself from being present in your life? Are you someone who lives in the future and is always thinking ahead, or are you living in the past, ruminating about past experiences?

2. For today, set an intention that you are going to be present for five consecutive minutes in your day. Go outside and allow yourself to be in nature for five minutes. This could be in your backyard, in a park, or even outside of where you work if you have limited options. Look around you and take in the sights and sounds. Do not look at your phone or any other distractions, simply allow yourself to be aware of your surroundings for five minutes. Take deep breaths in and out and breathe in the fresh air around you. At the end of five minutes, note how you feel compared to how you felt when you first started the exercise.

<u>Daily Mantra:</u>

"Every moment of my life is priceless."

Exercise 4: Overcoming Doubt

Cobwebs

Your inner spirit is one of trust and knowing. However, as you go through life and have difficult or challenging experiences, you may begin to doubt this inner knowledge. Distrust and fear can start to creep in due to past conditioning from others. You may begin to forget your inner worthiness and look outside of yourself for answers. Yet, the more you look outside of yourself for your own truth, the more that fear and doubt multiply. This fear settles and becomes a cobweb that lingers in your mind, causing you to distrust yourself. This fear will find the blackest, most isolated crevice in your mind, sit there, and wait. A cobweb hidden out of sight. In doing so, it can be in the periphery, not in your direct conscious thought. By staying concealed, fear is able to influence you in a subtle way. It casts an ominous shadow over situations and interactions. Your self-image and perceptions become distorted and hazy. Decisions and change are seen as scary and threatening, as the doubt in the darkness is whispering to you that you cannot trust yourself and need outside validation.

Yet, it is possible to start to bring your fear into the light and lead a life of being empowered instead of hesitant. This takes some detective work on your part. It can be difficult to detect the fear in your mind, as with time it becomes ingrained in your thought process. Instead of trying to sift through every thought you have to find the fear, focus on your mood instead. Fear and doubt lower your mood by dripping their oily poison into your thoughts, which darkens your emotional state. Feeling sad, anxious, or angry is an opportunity to look deeper and expose the fear inside.

The best thing you can do to overcome fear is to deal with it directly. Fear and doubt do not like to be brought to light, as by working covertly, they keep you from remembering that you are a being of light and clarity. However, once you become aware enough to realize that your thoughts are being altered by fear, you can make a different choice for yourself. Your conscious thought, what you are focusing on and aware of, is a powerful device.

You can use your consciousness—your awareness—like a beam of light inside your mind to expose the lingering doubtfulness and fear. This brilliant beam can be powerful when it is fueled by love and self-worth. Bring forward the fear thoughts that are stealing your joy. Remind yourself that thoughts are just thoughts, not reality or truth. Reject the thoughts that are fear-based and place them into this beam of love and allow them to evaporate. Replace your doubt and fear with love and trust. Trust yourself that you are capable and can overcome adversity. Trust in Spirit that you are connected to a greater energy that is your ally. Project your beam of light deep within and aim for the dark corners that are slowly stealing your joy. Let this light clear out the mustiness that remains tucked away in the depth of your existence. As negative thoughts emerge, place them in the light and let them fade away into nothingness. You may have to do this repeatedly, as fear-based thoughts can be stubborn and might spring up when you are confronted with adversity, but remember that your beam of light is always ready to shine. Your conscious thought can be stronger than any limiting belief if you choose to activate it with love. Keep your own self-worth always in your awareness.

You can also work on warding off future, fear-based thoughts. Set an intention for this beam of worthiness and love to glow inside of you like a shining star indefinitely. Let the star's light penetrate into all of your mind's cracks and crevices. Imagine this light beaming so brightly for you that the fear has nowhere to retreat. It is fully exposed now and does not have the power to influence you, as it cannot penetrate the star's brilliance. Trust in the stamina of your protecting star. You are now safe and can believe in yourself as you were meant to. Live from this place of trust and love long enough and you become the star, as you are a being of light and love. Know that you are strong enough to remove all darkness.

<u>Reflection Questions/Exercises:</u>

1. In what ways do you doubt yourself? How has fear and doubt limited your life?

2. For today, sit in a quiet, meditative state for 10-15 minutes. You may want to set a timer to go off at the allotted time, or you may choose to just do the meditation experience until it feels right for you to stop. To start, sit in a comfortable position and try to limit interruptions. Close your eyes and start to take slow, deep breaths. Focus on your breathing, inhaling and exhaling. Now, imagine a beam of light in your mind. This beam is fueled by your own self-worth and love, and is strong. Allow this light to shine brightly in your mind, banishing darkness. Picture it evaporating your negative, doubting, self-limiting thoughts into nothing. Continue to sit with that image while you are slowing breathing in and out until the end of the meditation. During your meditation experience, if you find yourself getting distracted, focus back on your breathing until you feel centered again, and then continue with your exercise. Journal afterward about any emotions or resistance that came up for you during this experience.

<u>Daily Mantra:</u>

"I trust my inner light to lead me to positive outcomes."

Exercise 5: Relationships

Investments

Energy is universal and exists in all things. You have personal energy that flows through you and around you every day. The environment and people who you encounter can impact this dynamic flow. The interpersonal connections between you and others are a web of energy, always in motion. This energy give-and-take is similar to monetary transactions. When you give love and encouragement to others, you are making a positive investment for yourself. Your words not only uplift others but also raise your own vibrational frequency. You increase your emotional assets by showing compassion to those around you. Being gentle and kind to yourself is another way to increase your emotional abundance. Love opens the door to emotional prosperity all around.

However, each time that you judge another or engage in gossiping or complaining, your positive energy decreases. Although it is likely not your intention to do so, your criticism or complaining invests and connects you into the person or situation that you are unhappy with. This negative energy ties you like a rope to the unwanted situation or difficulty, which then lowers your frequency, slowing draining your emotional wealth. This is the same as sinking your hard-earned money into a financial investment that is doomed to fail. Your righteousness and entitlement cloud your vision, and you do not see the danger in the investment. You only see your perception that you are justified in your opinions and look no deeper. Meanwhile, your personal energy assets start to diminish. This is the same as going bankrupt financially.

It is not possible to avoid every negative person or to never have a situation that is displeasing to you. As life happens, you will encounter challenges that give you a choice as to how you are going to respond. You always have options as to how you are going to "spend" your personal energy. You could invest in love and forgive others, or you can speak harshly and cast judgments. While other people's actions are out of your control, your own actions belong solely to you. You are your own banker, no one else's. It is not your life task to assess and criticize everyone else's behavior, energy, or assets. Release yourself from the burden of feeling that things outside of your control need your opinion and judgment. Disentangle yourself from other people's depreciating emotional investments. Let others be in charge of their own emotional health.

Focus on increasing your own investments by choosing love and forgiveness. Just as you would in business, be deliberate in which people and situations you choose to invest. Enhance your portfolio by being loving towards others and refraining from judgments and criticism. Remember that your actions and words will direct where your own emotional investments will settle, and the value that they will hold. Allow your words to create abundance for yourself and others by investing in thoughts and actions that have the highest payout—kindness.

<u>Reflection Questions/Exercises:</u>

1. Evaluate your personal energy investments. What kinds of words do you exchange with others? Do you spend a lot of time investing in negativity or do you promote positivity with your words?

2. For today, pay special attention to the words that you speak to the people you encounter. Set an intention that you are going to be careful with your words and actions. Make a conscious effort to speak kindly and resist the urge to complain and criticize. If a difficult situation does come up, acknowledge it for what it is—a difficult situation—and nothing more. Resist the urge to give the challenging situation more power by complaining or perseverating on it. Give yourself positive feedback each time you are able to move forward without investing a piece of yourself into a difficult situation. Notice if this changes your mood and emotional tone throughout your day by reflecting on how you feel at the end of the exercise.

<u>Daily Mantra:</u>

"I speak in a loving way, towards myself and others."

Exercise 6: Acceptance

A Lone Path

A human life is one of connections. These connections come from relationships and experiences. Many crucial interactions happen early on in life, such as the relationship that a child has with his parents or caretakers. A child learns about the world and his place in it from his parent's actions and words.

A vital parenting role is to make children feel that they are loved, valued, and safe. However, many parents are not able to provide this love and nurturing to their children for whatever reason. Parents may be unable to love themselves and have limited love to offer anyone else, and thus, this lack is passed along to their child. This results in a child growing up and feeling incomplete, deficient, or unsafe, and living from a fear-based perspective. Going through life this way is difficult. This child grows to be an adult who learns to use coping skills to deal with the lack of love. Sometimes this involves self-medicating with drugs or alcohol to numb the feeling of being unlovable. Others may become perfectionists to protect themselves against future rejection by trying to never behave in a way that would be seen as undesirable. Perhaps a person may put up a barrier between himself and the world, to keep people at a distance, as the child in him still remembers the feeling of being rejected and unloved, and strives to keep all possible rejections at a distance. These patterns and defense mechanisms can go on indefinitely, demand much energy, and steal much joy out of life.

Know that there is another way to approach life, even if you are someone who came from a challenging background. Yet, having a different mindset requires that you examine a few truths. The events in your past cannot be changed. There is nothing that can be done now that will erase the painful memories from your past. Know that you are no longer a helpless child. You are now a capable adult and have the luxury of being in charge of your own future. You are not dependent on others to meet your emotional needs. You are able to open up your perspective to new possibilities.

It is helpful to think of your life as a path that began when you were born and will physically end when you die. If you had parents that did not meet your needs, you might harbor resentment towards them, that they did not fulfill their duty. That they selfishly walked ahead of you on your path, not looking back, while your little legs hurried to catch them. Your eager hands were hungry for their touch or comfort, and you may believe that your parents withheld it from you purposefully, leaving you grasping. This is a perception that invokes loneliness and may have given you the impression that you were somehow left behind on the highway of life.

However, consider the following alternative. Your parents have never left you behind, as they have never set foot on your path. You walk on a solo path from the time you enter this earth. You are currently on a lone path, not a main walkway that everyone travels on. Your feet are the only ones that have ever tread on your particular avenue. Your parents and other people all walk a solo trail also. As a child, your path started out parallel to others. This is because a human child cannot live alone for many years, needing nourishment and protection. Yet, as time went on, your path and your parents' path started to drift apart, the distance in between the trails widening. As a child, you may have seen this as being abandoned and forgotten. Yet, it is the natural course of life for all paths to take twists and turns in a totally unique way. Accepting this truth does not excuse or condone any past hurts that happened to you. Just because you are on a lone path does not invalidate or lessen any of the traumas or difficulties that you endured in the past. However, it does allow you to see that this past hurt does not have to live on your path anymore unless you choose to continue to allow it to. You are free now, there is no one forcing you to believe or to do anything further. Your path is completely your own, no one else's.

Remember that you cannot change how your parents chose to raise you. Their actions, their own path, directed yours for the majority of your childhood. Then you were left to direct your own path, only knowing the directions that you had come to follow, operating on a set of principles that you were taught. Looking back with bitterness in your heart for your parents misses the point. They were fulfilling their role in your lifetime to allow you to come to this juncture. They provided you the early experiences (both good and bad) that have made you the person you are now. You are exactly the person now that you need to be. You are able to see your life differently moving forward if you choose to. You can see your path ahead and you are in total control of it. Believe that your path is special and unique. Believe that your path matters. There are likely other paths closely linked to yours, but none that is going exactly where yours will end up. Paths are both separate and intertwined, infinite and personal, a massive network of existence.

To accept that you are alone on your path may initially seem isolating. But, remember that it is an illusion that you are ever "alone." Inside of your physical body lies an inner spirit that is connected to all life. A piece of Spirit, which is the universal life source, lives inside of you. This unites you to every other living thing. Spirit is not only holding your hand along the path, Spirit is the path. It is every stone along the way. It is in every space around you. Spirit loved you when you chose to start this journey. Spirit was there when you were scared, rejected, and alone, helping to keep your foot on your path, providing you a basis to move forward.

Realizing that you walk your own path is the ultimate creative freedom. You literally have the power to take your pathway anywhere. Love yourself enough to quit looking back. It is hard to see the possible future opportunities with your focus to the rear. Allow yourself to move forward now, and see your path clearly for what it truly is, a gift from Spirit.

<u>Reflection Questions/Exercises:</u>

1. When you imagine that you are on a lone path, what emotions does this bring up for you? Are there certain people that you are holding responsible for your current position in life? How would your outlook for the future change if you believed that you were in sole control of your destiny?

2. For today, sit in a quiet, meditative state for 10-15 minutes. You may want to set a timer to go off at the allotted time, or you may choose to just do the meditation experience until it feels right for you to stop. To start, sit in a comfortable position and try to limit interruptions. Close your eyes and take slow, deep breaths. Focus on your breathing, inhaling and exhaling. Next, visualize yourself standing on a lone path that was made just for you. Look around and take in the details of your surroundings. Remember that you are safe and loved on your path, as your path is from Spirit. Continue to breathe in and out and sit with the fact that you are only responsible for yourself on this path. Allow whatever feelings or thoughts this triggers to come forward. If it is an emotional response, let the response happen. During your meditation experience, if you find yourself getting distracted, focus back on your breathing until you feel centered again, and then continue with your exercise. Journal afterward about any emotions or resistance that came up for you during this experience.

<u>Daily Mantra:</u>

"My path is solely my own and full of potential."

Exercise 7: Parenting

The Value of Children

Having a child is one of the most profound experiences that one can have. Children have pure golden energy when they come into this life. They are physically dependent on their parents, but in other ways, know so much more. They have a connection to Spirit that is more on the surface, easier to tap into. As such, they radiate pure love. They look to you, their parents and caretakers, with this undiluted love. They really do not ask for more in this world than to be loved.

Love is the answer to all parenting questions. When children act out, they are eager for love, looking for attention. They want to see your eyes turn to them. Your eyes are deep, and your spirit connection can most easily be seen there. Through your eyes, you can connect with your child's spirit as your eyes tell the story that your mouth struggles to say. Use your eyes to tell your child the wonder and beauty that you see in them. Make time to look at your child. Really connect with their eyes and hold their gaze. Allow your inner spirit's golden light to fill up in your hands and fingers and touch your child's face. These things speak to a child in a way that words never could.

Children's spirits are pure, joyful, and full of life. A child's spirit has more of the memory for why they came to this place. To explore, to give, to receive love, and to touch another's spirit. They are not bogged down with expectations and conditioning that comes with years of experience. A child's eyes reflect the pure love that is within.

It is important to reach out to your child through visual connection but also through touch. A child craves your embrace. A child's spirit, being unimpeded and more accessible, can feel love through an embrace in a way that adults often do not. However, notice how amazing it feels when your child touches your face. Their soul is reaching out to you.

Spirit has a plan for your child that has nothing to do with you. Your job is to support and nourish your child's authentic self during their upbringing. Give them love and encouragement, help them flourish. Build them up with love. Make them feel worthy. The first person that they test their worthiness out on is you. Do not fail at this and ignore, diminish, or reject their eager hands and eyes, looking to you for validation of their place on this earth. That is all you have to do. Keep your intention as one of validation and love without conditions. Your own spirit is vast enough to both live your life's purpose and to support your child while they are coming into theirs.

Raising children is a reminder from Spirit that you also possess the same precious inner spirit as your child. Look at yourself with the same loving gaze that you bestow on your child. Your child is looking to you for confirmation of their worth, but they also have the intention to help you love yourself as well.

Children's spirits recognize that you are a soul in need of help also. Accept the love from your child. That is a gift from Spirit. A precious reminder that you are also valued, loved, and treasured by the one who made you. By the one who made all life.

<u>Reflection Questions/Exercises:</u>

1. If you interact with children in your life, what are your interactions like? Are you able to connect with your child in an authentic way? What barriers or distractions get in the way? Is spending time with your children a priority for you?

2. For today, set an intention to spend 20 minutes with your child and give them your undivided attention. Make good eye contact with your child and make a point to hug them or touch them affectionately. Remove all distractions of telephone, television, and computers. Allow your child to direct the conversation or activity and notice the quality of this interaction. Notice how your child responds to this and how you feel after engaging with them in this way.

<u>Daily Mantra:</u>

"I respond to my child with love and validation."

Exercise 8: Releasing Limitations

Concerts

Every human life is unique and separate; however, it is also connected to the past—to your family's heritage and genealogy. You move forward on your path independently, yet past experiences that you and your family's ancestors have lived is part of the background in your daily existence. The lives that your grandparents led influence your own life, as their parenting influenced your own parents, who influenced you.

The impact your distant relatives have had on your day-to-day life is sometimes hard to detect, as you may not even have known the people who are influencing your life now. You may hold certain beliefs about the world and your place in it that are not related to actual experiences you have had. You may hold grudges or have negative perceptions of groups of people based on past experiences that your family lived through. As a child, you hear your family's comments and judgments about things and absorb that into your own perception of the world. These prejudices possibly have been present for so long that you may not even be consciously aware of them. However, each belief that you hold impacts how your day-to-day reality will look. If you feel that the world is unsafe, things will happen around you that reinforce that belief. If you harbor resentment against a certain group of people, your mind will look for negative facts about this group that will strengthen your belief. Your mind is always looking to substantiate ideas that it already holds as truths, to further solidify the perceptions that it operates on.

It is important to take the time to review the biases and prejudices that you hold as truths for yourself. Examine where these beliefs come from. Is it from an actual experience that you had with someone or something, or is this a belief placed in your mind when you were a child? Your opinions and perceptions hold a significant amount of weight, as they influence your choices and actions.

These conditioned thoughts and perceptions become the orchestra that is playing in the background of your life. Your perceptions and beliefs are the instruments, each creating a sound that has an influence over your choices and actions. You may live an entire lifetime and not even be aware that there are instruments playing. The sounds can be loud or soft, harsh or cohesive. It varies depending on each situation and experience. Becoming aware that this orchestra exists is the first step in living a more empowered existence. Look at the instruments that are playing, what kind of beliefs do you hold about yourself and the world around you? What is the overall sound of the instruments? Supportive? Loving? Negative? Judgmental? Examine where these beliefs—these sounds—are stemming from. Are your perceptions based on facts, or on thoughts that you were mistaking for facts?

The next step to changing the background music is to become aware that you are the conductor of these instruments. You are not a passive member of the audience. You have the ultimate control over the sounds that the instruments produce. As these instruments are playing the melody of your life, it would be wise to spend some time tuning them. You have the power to alter the quality of sound from harsh to harmonious. However, changing the quality of your melody requires a practice of stillness in order to hear each note clearly. Allow yourself the space to hear the noises for what they are—perceptions. You then have the freedom to organize the instruments and teach them a song that enhances your life. Remember that you are a being that is worthy of having an amazing symphony supporting you at all times.

Likely, your history has some undertones of regret and sadness, as all lives do. There are difficult and tragic times in all lives. As you cannot change the past, these instruments will be present regardless. However, you are not doomed to listen to screeching discord. These difficult past experiences only add depth to your chorus, as every orchestra has a mix of soft and tender sounds as well as deep, bass tones.

Choose to be empowered in your life and challenge your perceptions. You always have the option to change your beliefs, no matter what kind of background you came from. Decide to move from the audience to the stage. Pick up your baton; hold it up in the air and conduct. Begin your work of art, the triumphant symphony known as you.

<u>Reflection Questions/Exercises:</u>

1. Reflect on what beliefs you are currently holding in your life that may be limiting the ways you interact with the world. Are there grudges, biases, or prejudices that you have against others or about certain situations? Review where these perceptions originated. Are you basing your thoughts on facts or on past conditioning? What would be another way to think about these situations that would open you up more to life's opportunities?

2. Set an intention today to pick one limiting belief you hold about others or yourself. Examples could be, "people can't be trusted," or "the world is an unsafe place." This limiting belief may also be about a certain person or group of people that you deem as "bad, inferior, or less than." Challenge yourself to look for positive things that disprove this belief. If you feel that others are not trustworthy or are against you in some way, look instead for experiences of people supporting each other and acting as helpers in the community. Examine if your limiting belief currently is substantiated by facts in your life or are you projecting your own perceptions outward? Allow your mind to think about this situation in a different way and open yourself up to a new possibility.

<u>Daily Mantra:</u>

"My beliefs about myself and others are supportive and enrich my life."

Exercise 9: Worthiness

Spotlights

There are many opportunities for growth in life. There are many different projects and goals that you could choose to give time and attention to. This is part of the diversity and free will that this human experience offers. Some people may look at these projects or experiences as a means to an end. People who are very results-focused and future thinking often have a hard time living in the now moment. They are always looking ahead to see what needs to be done. They rarely take the time to appreciate a finished project, instead moving on to the next.

Think of getting a stage ready for a performance. There are many projects to do—building sets, getting the lighting just right, making costumes, and adjusting the sound. You may see your life as a production that is a never-ending list of tasks. You may be working tirelessly to make something beautiful and meaningful, but end up living backstage, too busy to allow yourself to shine in the spotlight.

Furthermore, you may be someone who is anxious to have "all eyes on you." Perhaps you avoid the spotlight for fear that if you were to stand there, you would open yourself up to criticism and judgments. You may feel that backstage is a safer location, as you can blend in and not bring any attention to yourself. Or, you could avoid the spotlight due to feeling that you are not worthy or not good enough to stand in a place that is meant for someone special to shine.

Yet, remember this, you did not choose to come to Earth to live a life in the shadows. Every person is meant to be center stage in the production that is his or her life. Appreciate what you already have built;

your stage is currently perfect just as it is. Take the time right now to stop and allow yourself to step into the center of the stage. Step into the spotlight and stay there. Just see how it feels. It is warm, bright, and inviting.

If the thought of being on stage in front of an audience is scary to you, remember this, there is no one in the audience but you. You are not putting on a production for the masses. You are not living a life so that others can weigh in and determine your worth. You are living a solo experience for your own spirit's growth and exploration. The audience is not full of other people watching you. It is full of you's. A hundred you's all sitting in the auditorium and watching you with admiring eyes. They are so proud of you and for what you have already done. They want you to spend more time in the spotlight, to stop running and let their love pour on to you. They feel you are perfect just as you are. They forgive you for the mistakes you have made in the past. They want you to release your negative perceptions of yourself and just "be" the perfect version of you that you are right now.

Enjoy this place and accept this love and encouragement. The spotlight is yours for as long as you want it. Do not feel that you have to rush away or that you do not deserve to stand there. Come back to it anytime you need, to be reminded of your worth and accomplishments. You may step away from it eventually, as there will always be projects and goals to work on in life, but remember that this spotlight is yours and always open to you. Your life is a beautiful production, and you are the star.

<u>Reflection Questions/Exercises:</u>

1. What kind of experience are you currently living? Are you the star of your own show, or do you hide backstage? What are your beliefs about being in the spotlight and having attention focused on you?

2. For today, sit in a quiet, meditative state for 10-15 minutes. You may want to set a timer to go off at the allotted time, or you may choose to just do the meditation experience until it feels right for you to stop. To start, sit in a comfortable position and try to limit interruptions. Close your eyes and start to take slow, deep breaths. Focus on your breathing, inhaling and exhaling. Now imagine the scene that was previously discussed. Imagine yourself standing on a stage and that the auditorium seats are full of you's, all clapping and beaming at how amazing you are. Sit with this image and see if you can hold it. Allow the love of the audience to fill you up as you continue to take deep breaths in and out. During your meditation experience, if you find yourself getting distracted, focus back on your breathing until you feel centered again, and then continue with your exercise. If this visualization triggers any resistance or negative feelings from you, journal about those feelings after meditation and explore them further.

<u>Daily Mantra:</u>

"My life is a beautiful production, and I am the star."

Exercise 10: Acceptance

Sandcastles

The human existence can be mysterious and unpredictable. Change comes and goes. Things that were once stable can be taken or lost, and your life is impacted forever. No life is without some hardship and grief. It can be difficult to accept that change and loss are always possible. Yet, fighting against change, living from a place of fear and resistance, will not alter the fact that the course of your life can be redirected at any moment. It is meaningful work to look at these truths and still have the courage to go on living and loving others.

One powerful tool is to live life in the present moment, knowing that it is fleeting, knowing that it is fragile. Think of the fragile sand that creates a sandcastle. Each grain of sand is a small moment in your life. A series of "now" moments that combine to make your sandcastle, which is your current existence.

There is no guarantee that any castle is safe on the beach. It is possible that an ocean wave could come crashing in at any moment. This wave could hit as the castle is just getting started, it could barely be off the ground. Or, a wave could hit a fully built castle, with layers upon layers of detail. All castles—all lives—are vulnerable, no matter how meticulously they have been created. Eventually, a wave will come and bring all the sand back—all the lives—back to the ocean.

This thought may seem alarming, as the human mind fears things that are unpredictable; however, impermanence is a universal truth. Also, remember that your current human life is but one small extension of the eternal spirit that lives inside of you. Your true self is an infinite being that cannot be destroyed or damaged. Accepting this fact allows you to see your human life with some perspective. There is nothing to fear, as when this physical life is over, you will return to the life source of Spirit, which is an ocean of pure love.

For now, you are a castle in the sand, but your inner spirit knows that you extend far beyond that which is found on the beach. Your physical experience is one that is meant to be lived fully. Have the conscious intention to utilize your time abundantly, loving freely, and trusting Spirit's plan for you.

If you have ever built a real sandcastle before, you know that the best sand to use is partly damp sand. It helps the whole structure stick together better. This sand can be found closest to the ocean shore. Notice that this sand could also be considered the most vulnerable, as it lives in a place of unpredictability. The ocean is near, and your human mind could see this as a threat. However, the truth is that you are also closest to the life source, the ocean. This is the home of Spirit, and if allowed, Spirit will work tirelessly in your life to support you and keep your castle solid.

You may feel that dry sand is safer to use, as you are as far away from the ocean as possible, assuming that this will minimize the chance of change happening. However, castles built in this way are crumbly, prone to blowing over with a gust of wind. This is a life lived in an anxious state, always anticipating "what will happen next," and not appreciating the beauty of the current moment. A life lived in this way misses the magnificence that the beach has to offer. And, the truth remains the same that all sand will eventually return to the ocean no matter if it is currently dry or not.

Notice the sand that surrounds you each day, the meaningful things that are present in your daily life. Accepting that your time on this earth is not guaranteed makes it easier to appreciate your now moments—each grain of sand—as you are aware that each instant could be your last, which makes each moment precious.

Yes, it is accepting that change and loss are always possibilities to build your castle in the wet sand by the shoreline. Yes, it can be scary to live life in the current moment, to be willing to love another, and to accept being vulnerable, but a solid castle makes for a rewarding life. A castle that is accepting when its time comes to rejoin Spirit in the vastness of the ocean, deep and eternal.

<u>Reflection Questions/Exercises:</u>

1. Explore your level of acceptance with not being in control of situations and your attitude towards change. What emotions surface for you when you think about the impermanence of life? In what ways do you try to exert control over situations and other people? How do you think your life would be different if you accepted change and impermanence as truths and did not fight them?

2. For today, set a timer for one minute and sit quietly wherever you are. This can be at work on a break, at home, or sitting outside. For one minute, just focus on your breathing and be still. Breathe in and out and feel the air moving in, then out of your lungs. Look around and take in the details of your surroundings. Pay attention to how your body feels in this exact moment. Notice the beauty that is living in this moment in time. Appreciate the fact that you are seeing this beauty and are currently alive on this earth.

Notice how your body feels after this minute is over. Assess your emotional state and see if anything feels different compared to how you felt before you started this exercise. Repeat this exercise two more times today, in a variety of locations and situations. It may help to journal afterward about the experiences you had during this time of reflection.

<u>Daily Mantra:</u>

"I live life in the present moment, appreciating the beauty that exists all around me."

Exercise 11: Releasing Limitations

Life Gardens

Think of your life as a garden and you are the gardener. There is a large field with crops growing all around you. These crops are the beliefs about yourself that you hold. Your garden—your beliefs—have been cultivated by you and others your whole life. You live in the environment that the fields create; you eat the produce that the crops yield. It is important to notice that most of your crop was planted early on. Your parents and other early influential figures in your life planted the seeds that formed the framework of your current garden. Your parents planted your seeds based on what they knew to be best at the time. They planted seeds based on their own beliefs and perceptions.

Yet, as you continue throughout your life, you may notice that some things have been growing that are not enhancing your garden, beliefs, which are not supporting your life. You may have a whole section of radishes growing even though you hate radishes. But, instead of removing them and using that space for something else, you keep it around since other people like radishes and have told you that a "real garden" has radishes. Radishes can represent a variety of things, working at a job that you hate, playing a certain "role" that you have no passion for, holding on to a relationship that is unfulfilling, or engaging in behaviors that are self-limiting. Even though you do not feel fulfilled by these things, you may continue to keep them in your life, as you feel that is what is expected of you.

Many people go throughout life and do not even notice the crops they are surrounded by. This is an unconscious way of living that leaves your fate up to the beliefs that have been planted by others.

Choose to make a different experience for yourself. Look around and take notice of the plants that surround you and begin to assess the beliefs that are fueling your daily existence. What beliefs are you feeding yourself that are enhancing your life? Which beliefs are limiting you? Begin to think about what your ideal garden would look like. How would you like the crops around you to support your life?

Start to trust your own voice and your own abilities as a gardener. Any possibility can happen when you begin to grow self-affirming beliefs. Get out the shovel and dig out the areas that are no longer working for you. Throw them away, over the fence and do not think twice about it. Begin to sow the following: "I am worthy." "My life matters." "I am capable." Plant any other beliefs that speak to your heart and bring passion to your life. Remember that you are growing the produce solely for yourself, so you do not need to check in with anyone else before planting beliefs that enhance your existence.

Tend to your seeds daily, giving them love and nourishment. Allow yourself to flourish on the healthy produce your crops yield. Fill up on what inspires you and keeps your soul vibrant, as this garden is the scenery for your life.

<u>Reflection Questions/Exercises:</u>

1. What are you growing in your garden that is limiting your potential? What seeds have you planted yourself that are limiting? What seeds have others planted? What beliefs do you hold that are currently working well for you?

2. For today, take 20 minutes to sit down and draw out your ideal garden with you in the middle. Around you, write four or five beliefs that you would like to "plant" about yourself. Place these positive beliefs in sections around you, just as you would do for planting different seeds. Examples of beliefs could be "I am fulfilled in my job," or "I am a loving parent." Then, under the positive belief, write down several steps you could take today to start making these beliefs a reality. Under your "being a more loving parent" section, this may be things like "spend at least 30 minutes a day of one-on-one time with my child with no distractions," or "instead of immediately responding to my child with yelling, stop and breathe for 10 seconds, then respond." Add color or anything else that makes this piece of art stand out for you. Now hang this sketch up where you can see it daily and then look at it to remind yourself of the positive beliefs that you would like to have to enhance your life. Say the beliefs aloud every day and start to believe them about yourself.

<u>Daily Mantra:</u>

"I am the master gardener of my own existence."

Exercise 12: Worthiness

Cages

Many people struggle with a false perception that they are unlovable or "bad" in some way. It is lonely to live in this place of feeling unworthy of love. You suffer as you ask only for what you feel you deserve. To ask for almost no love means that at some level you feel you deserve none.

Another common experience is to look outside of yourself for things that you think will make you feel worthy, or to look for validation from others that you are important. You may be so dependent on assurance from others that you are lovable that when someone rejects you or disapproves of you in some way, it crushes you emotionally. This is a difficult way to live, as your opinion of yourself is reliant on another's opinion.

Think of an animal raised in a zoo in a controlled environment. The animal lives in a cage waiting for someone else to take care of it, dependent on others for its survival. The animal is trapped in a cage and has no free will to change its environment.

Feeling that you are unlovable is similar to being an animal that sits in a cage. You are waiting for someone to reach out to you in a way that makes you feel loved. You are waiting for another to feed you, to give you the reassurance that you are worthy and accepted. You do not have the confidence that you can do anything else and feel that your potential is limited. Believing that all your possibilities for love reside in the space that is your cage. Holding the belief that there will never be anything more than this, never looking past the bars in front of you.

The belief that you are unworthy can impact your entire existence; however, it does not have to be this way. Contemplate an alternative view of the situation. Consider that there are no bars in front of you, as there is no cage. You only believed that you were limited and thus imprisoned yourself into a narrow box of possibilities. The bars that you see in front of you are your own restrictive perceptions manifesting in a variety of ways that looks confining. It is an illusion that there is something lacking within you, or that there is something that another person can give you that will make you whole. It is transformative to wake up to the reality that you are actually a free being. You are free to leave the confines you have been stuck in for so long. You are free to enter the wilderness and seek out your own sustenance.

Every person has the tools needed to feed themselves. Reflect on the fact that an animal does not ask if it is worthy before it devours food it has found. There is no question for an animal, who trusts its natural ability to find food and nourishment. When an animal is free in the wild, it can do what nature intended it to do. The same is true for you. You have the capacity to fill yourself up with nourishing thoughts. Loving yourself is the key to being able to live independently.

As you begin to live from a place of sustaining yourself, you may notice that other people react differently to you. Often when there is a period of spiritual growth or an internal perception shift, there is also an outer change that manifests in your life. As you leave your cage and start to make your way to the wilderness of unlimited opportunities, you may notice some resistance from others. You might pass by people who are in similar self-imposed cages who are not used to seeing someone walking about freely. Many people choose to remain in their cages out of fear. These people may have liked it better when you were boxed in, knowing that you were someone who asked for very little. Feeling a sense of control that you were stuck in a cage like them, as this is predictable and "safe." People who do not have the capacity yet to love another without conditions, or who are unwilling to love themselves, may not be able to transition with you into your new lifestyle. That is okay. You are not on this earth to convince anyone that you are worthy of love, other than convincing yourself. These people will fall away as you get closer to the wilderness and as you leave behind the rigid perceptions of what you knew your life to be.

Prepare to be amazed by the things that happen next. There is no way to imagine what wonders lie up ahead. You are out of the cage and are free. You are no longer confined and limited. Everything you need, and more, awaits you.

<u>Reflection Questions/Exercises:</u>

1. In what ways do you look to others for validation? What power do you give others over your own emotional health in doing this? What self-perceptions do you hold about your own worthiness?

2. For today, sit in a quiet, meditative state for 10-15 minutes. You may want to set a timer to go off at the allotted time, or you may choose to just do the meditation experience until it feels right for you to stop. To start, sit in a comfortable position and try to limit interruptions. Close your eyes and start to take slow, deep breaths. Focus on your breathing, inhaling and exhaling. Hold your hands over your heart and quietly say the following mantra to yourself repeatedly, "I love myself completely, I am worthy." Continue to repeat this mantra and feed yourself love quietly until the meditation time ends. During your meditation experience, if you find yourself getting distracted, focus back on your breathing until you feel centered again, and then continue with your exercise. If this visualization triggers any resistance or negative feelings from you, journal about those feelings after meditation and explore them further.

<u>Daily Mantra:</u>

"I love myself enough to choose a life of freedom."

Exercise 13: Mindfulness

Headphones

For many people, day-to-day life is hectic and fast paced. There are many things competing for your attention at once. Interactions and experiences are happening rapidly. You may feel that you are present in your life, as you physically are having these experiences. However, being physically present in your life is not the same as being mentally present.

Think of seeing your life as a movie being played out on a screen. You are watching yourself in action, doing your daily tasks and routines. Now imagine that instead of hearing the soundtrack of the movie and what is actually being said, you have headphones on and are listening to something entirely different. Instead of accurately hearing the sounds of your film, you are listening to a pre-recorded set of statements that are playing over and over. This is your internal dialog that is based on perceptions, habituation, and past experiences.

It is normal to have an inner voice that appraises your experiences throughout the day. This voice uses your memories to help you make sense of the world around you. It is looking to the past to see what kind of experience is similar to what is happening now. It is looking to the future to see what it should suggest next. This is an essential part of living, for your mind needs to be able to make connections and link things together.

Yet, this voice can get put on hyperdrive, constantly in the background making judgments and comments, determining what "should or should not" be happening. Fueling your emotions by triggering chemical reactions based on perceptions of what is "good" or "bad." It is rare that this voice is able to stay in the current moment and just be with the situation without judgment, yet that is the path to enriching your life and living authentically. The more you are able to quiet this internal dialogue, the more you are able to truly be aware of what your life is at this moment.

The first step is to be cognizant of what your internal dialogue sounds like. You may not even be aware that you have headphones on. You may think that you are watching the movie and hearing things accurately. However, if your internal voice is going at full force, it is impossible to truly hear what is being said around you.

Work on noticing when that internal voice is loud and judgmental. What it is saying? Usually, this voice is casting your perceptions and expectations outward on to others. The best way to work on silencing this voice is to become aware of it, then to practice sitting quietly, as one does in meditation. It takes time to learn to quiet your mind. It takes effort to change your mindset from one of a noisy, internal voice to one of a quiet observer. However, it is possible to live this way. Begin to practice this in small ways every day. When someone is telling you something, try to not think about your response, just hear the message. You do not have to immediately respond to everything that is said. You can sit quietly and hear it, think for a moment, then respond. When situations come up in your everyday life, observe what is happening from a place of peace and calm. Allow yourself to pause, and then react. Work on removing the headphones and listening to the "real" soundtrack that is happening in your existence.

As you go throughout your day, think about if you are wearing your headphones or authentically engaging, as being fully present is when the true magic happens. There are amazing things to hear if you can sit quietly and listen to the sounds of your life, which are playing all around you.

<u>Reflection Questions/Exercises:</u>

1. What kind of dialog plays in your mind daily? After reading the above, do you feel you are actively participating in your life or are you living mostly in your mind?

2. For today, practice having authentic encounters with the people and the situations in your life. While you are engaging with others, or when you are going throughout your daily routine, notice if you are truly listening and aware of the situation or if you are making judgments in your head and preoccupied. If you are not truly listening to the current moment, become aware of the types of things that your inner voice is trying to distract you with. Notice if any critical or judgmental thoughts come up about other people and situations. Practice allowing these judgments to pass by you and return your focus again to what the situation is presenting to you. It may be helpful to set a reminder/alarm on your phone to go off at different times throughout the day. This alarm can remind you to check in at that moment and see if you are present and connected in the current moment, or if you are distracted by your thoughts. At the end of the day, journal about what patterns you noticed for yourself as the day progressed and explore these patterns further.

<u>Daily Mantra:</u>
"I engage authentically with the life I am living."

Exercise 14: Releasing Limitations

Starry Nights

You presently have a human existence that feels linear. You move from one day to the next, seeing the current image of yourself in the mirror each day. You may feel that this present-day version of yourself is the only version that is imaginable.

To believe this way is to live a life that places boundaries on your possibilities, instead of one that is open to a variety of outcomes. You likely are holding on to false beliefs that were placed in your mind by an outside source. This usually stems from childhood, when expectations and opinions were placed on you, influencing your self-perception. You are still operating from these beliefs, even if many are not in your conscious awareness. It is not necessarily a negative thing to hold certain perceptions about yourself. The human mind strives to make sense of things, comparing your own perceptions to the array of input that is received moment to moment. However, the problem begins when you do not allow your self-perception to be flexible and when you restrict yourself to only having one possible or acceptable outcome for your life.

These false, limiting perceptions narrow your vision and focus like a telescope narrows your sight to one specific target in the sky. The telescope is focused on one point in space, which is your current reality. As this is the truth that you see each day with your eyes, you may allow yourself to be stuck here. Never expanding the view of the telescope to see what else is existing in the space around you.

Yet, the truth is that you are a being of endless possibilities. You are currently living one version of your life. However, there are numerous versions that can exist, each as magnificent as the other. You have infinite potential to create anything you desire. You are not confined to any one particular outcome, belief, or experience. It is only your mind—your rigid beliefs about yourself—that narrows your focus to what you see around you each day. Enhancing your vision starts with expanding or letting go of the telescope. Put it down and look again at the night sky with your true eyes, which are the eyes of your spirit. See the fact that you are not only one solitary star but also every star that ever existed, all shining brilliantly.

Re-examine whatever beliefs you are telling yourself that are limiting. Challenge yourself to rediscover the multifaceted being that was given the opportunity to live the life you are currently living. Expand your awareness and begin to release these restrictive beliefs, setting a new intention for yourself that anything is possible. See yourself living the life that you desire. Imagine what it would feel like if this new reality existed and sit with that feeling. Cherish this sacred space and believe in it. Release the telescope that you have been mistaking for truth. Reject limitations and fear. Dismiss the belief that there are boundaries to your potential. Remember to expand your awareness and know that you are not only one star but also the entire starry sky. Full of wonder and possibility, you exist on the blanket of Spirit, which is vast, eternal, and supporting you always.

<u>Reflection Questions/Exercises:</u>

1. Ask yourself what you would like your life to be if any option was available to you. What are some goals and desires that you wish would come to fruition? What beliefs do you hold that block these possibilities from being able to appear? What small steps can you take today to start making your goals and dreams a reality?

2. For today, spend 10-15 minutes doing a visualization exercise. Get into a quiet, meditative state and try to limit distractions. Then imagine your life exactly as you wish it would be. See yourself living the life that you want for yourself. Visualize a scene from this reality. Add details and narrative to enhance the scene exactly to your liking. Afterward, journal about the experience and explore what emotions or thoughts were triggered for you.

<u>Daily Mantra:</u>

"My life is full of endless possibilities."

Exercise 15: Worthiness

Hunger Pains

Love is an essential component of a human life. Children especially crave love and are born being wide open to receiving loving energies from others. Love is as vital to overall health as nutritious food is, and children could eat heaping servings of love at every meal. Children have a strong need to feel wanted, cherished, heard, and protected. Yet, it is the unfortunate experience of many children not to get a full serving of love at each meal. Parents fail at times. They forget to serve love at breakfast, lunch, and dinner. They can be so distracted by duties, chores, and obligations, that serving three full meals of love every day is placed on the back burner, or forgotten about altogether.

You may have gone to sleep hungry for love numerous times as a child. This does not mean that your parents always failed to serve the meals. They may have served all they had to give, but it was not enough to satisfy your ravaging hunger. It can be an overwhelming job for parents to produce abundant, loving meals all day long. Many parents give all they have, and all they know to make, but a child can still feel lacking. Or, some parents are unable to provide love at all—even for themselves—so their children are left always wanting.

The love that children are served when they are young impacts the amount of love they feel they deserve moving forward. A child who is always hungry for love but never receives does not expect love from others and is often unable to see his own worth or lovability. This differs from a child who was surrounded by loving abundance, filled up on nourishing love every day. This child moves forward with the feeling that he deserves to have nourishment, and he will seek out sustenance for himself.

These truths can be hard to reflect back on and accept, yet the past is done. Your parents offered the love they had to share, whether this was enough to fill your young tummy or not. Looking forward, you are now in control of your own meals. It can be strange at first to remember that you have two capable hands. Two hands that can gather ingredients, turn on the stove, and feed you. You may have gone without for so long that you do not even notice the hunger pains anymore. This is the same as someone who goes throughout their life and does not feel worthy of love in any form. However, no one is so far removed from Spirit that they cannot come back to the place of noticing being hungry for love. Every person is capable of giving himself or herself the love that they need.

You must first remember that you are worthy of feeling full. You are lovable in all ways. You are worthy of eating until your heart is bursting. Start to practice this in your everyday life by slowly feeding yourself love. Choose to speak kindly to yourself instead of speaking harshly. Forgive yourself for your mistakes or missteps, and stop withholding loving meals from yourself as punishment. Challenge your false perceptions that you are someone who is not worthy of love. Imagine yourself as the small child who was looking to others for reassurance, who deserved to be loved in every way. You are just as deserving now. Cherish this child and serve them the meals that they needed then and that you still need now, as love is a vital nutrient for all.

<u>Reflection Questions/Exercises:</u>

1. Review your past experiences with having your need for love fulfilled as a child and adult. How have these experiences impacted your current feeling of worthiness? Are you someone who is open to love from others? Are you open to loving thoughts from yourself?

2. For today, practice the following exercise. See yourself as the small child that you used to be. Imagine this perfect child, who was deserving of abundant love. This child version of you is going to spend today with the adult-you. Allow yourself to move through your day and keep the image of this child close to you. The little you is going to sit next to you, go to work with you, do chores with you, etc. This child can also hear your thoughts as this child is you. Imagine that you are showing this child their worth in your eyes. They are looking to you for validation and love, how are you going to fulfill that? Speak to yourself kindly throughout the day. If you mess up, forgive yourself and show the child-you that mistakes do not determine worthiness. When you pass a mirror, give yourself a compliment. When you complete tasks throughout the day, give yourself a pat on the back and tell yourself what an amazing job you are doing at life today. Remember that the little-you is listening and is learning from what you say. If you find yourself speaking harshly to yourself, forgive yourself for this and remind both the adult-you and child-you that both of you are loveable. At the end of the day, journal about this experience. How did it feel to fill yourself up with love versus condemn yourself? If you noticed resistance to this exercise, explore those feelings further as well.

<u>Daily Mantra:</u>

"I fill myself up with loving thoughts as I am worthy of love in every way."

Exercise 16: Overcoming Doubt

Bubbles of Inspiration

Life is ever changing and is full of choices regarding situations, interactions, and experiences. You are faced with many decisions from the time you wake up to the time you go to bed at night. You may struggle at times to determine what course of action is right for you. At some level, a perception may be operating in the background telling you that you are someone who needs reassurance from others, which leads you to endlessly question your own choices. You may fret over what to do next, looking to others for guidance. This produces a frantic, anxious energy that makes your mind feel chaotic—like a rough storm on the water—with waves crashing and strong currents. The storm is fueled by your own insecurity and lack of trust in yourself. Your mind may feel so unsettled that looking for answers outside of you is the only option available.

Another common problem is feeling that something external needs to happen before you feel content—before you will allow yourself to feel safe and secure. This is a state of waiting, as you are depending on your outside reality to validate you so you can feel calm on the inside. Living life in this way is problematic, as external influences are largely not in your control. It is a tricky business to wait on someone else's actions before you feel happy, or to wait for a certain outcome to ease your troubled mind.

The only thing you ever truly have control over is your own mind and your own actions. It is an illusion that you can be saved by anyone except yourself. It is an illusion that you are helpless and need guidance from others. The reality is that you are the only one capable of making authentic decisions for yourself. Your mind does not have to be a chaotic storm. You can live from a place of trusting your own inner spirit.

Picture your mind as a still pond. Spirit, which is your own intuition and inner guidance, lives in this pond and is eager to offer advice, support, and love. This guidance is powerful and strong, but it cannot be heard clearly when the surface of the pond is choppy. Spirit's messages are like bubbles of inspiration that float to the surface of the pond. These bubbles are powerful but subtle at the same time. They can easily be missed unless you are looking into the pond directly to find them. Bubbles are hard to detect during a violent storm that makes the water unsettled. A chaotic mind does not see anything but a stormy pond. A quiet mind notices the small changes on the calm surface and is able to tap into this wisdom.

It does require practice to quiet your mind, but it is a worthwhile endeavor. Allow the waters of your awareness to settle. Reduce noisy distractions and practice stillness. Listen to what your inner spirit is telling you. Take notice of the guidance that Spirit is offering. This guidance could manifest in many ways, such as a soft nudge to take action, being given new opportunities, or having a change in perception.

Sit next to your quiet pond often. Look into your own waters to be comforted as Spirit is always with you, guiding and supporting you with tender wisdom. Spirit is pure love, and will always point you to the choices that are life enhancing and that are for your highest good.

<u>Reflection Questions/Exercises:</u>

1. How comfortable are you making decisions? Are you someone who trusts their own voice, or do you look to others for direction or reassurance? How is your life limited by not relying more on your own opinions and guidance?

2. For today, sit in a quiet, meditative state for 10-15 minutes. You may want to set a timer to go off at the allotted time, or you may choose to just do the meditation experience until it feels right for you to stop. To start, sit in a comfortable position and try to limit interruptions. Close your eyes and start to take slow, deep breaths. Focus on your breathing, inhaling and exhaling. Now think of one situation or decision that you are unsure about in your current life, and present this question to your inner spirit. Pose the question, release it, and then sit quietly and be alert for any images, guidance, or feelings that present themselves to you. During your meditation experience, if you find yourself getting distracted, focus back on your breathing until you feel centered again, and then continue with your exercise. Journal about this experience afterward and write down any information that came to you or any emotions that were brought up.

<u>Daily Mantra:</u>

"My mind is a still pond, full of wisdom and knowing."

Exercise 17: Worthiness

Cracks

The natural state of your inner spirit is love. Light and love reside in everyone. Yet, throughout life, fear can begin to seep in and weaken your mind and body. As you are weakened by doubt and fear, light can begin to escape. Sometimes light is removed, sometimes it is given away. Often it just escapes slowly—dissipating into the abyss around you, slipping through small cracks.

Cracks form when you feel that you are unlovable, when you give away your power to others by depending on outside sources for your sense of worthiness. Cracks grow each time you reinforce a negative perception you have about yourself—when you feel powerless, not good enough, or hopeless. With enough wear and tear in a lifetime, a person can become full of cracks—full of doubts and self-loathing. However, this does not have to be the case. It is possible to live a life that is full of vitality and grace. The first step is to patch up the crevices that leak out your light. The best tool to use for this is love. Use love as a fortifier. Love can heal the cracks. Fill up with positive feedback for yourself. Notice your achievements and accomplishments, and the beautiful things about yourself. Forgive your mistakes. Know that Spirit loves you no matter what. As you do this daily, you begin to seal your cracks one by one. Eventually, your light will stop escaping, and there will be more light inside of you than ever before.

If you are someone who has lived with many doubts and critical thoughts, this work can seem daunting; however, do not be discouraged. Self-acceptance is a major life task that many have to work on. Every person has areas of their life where they lose energy and power to some degree. It is not "wrong" to continue to have some cracks that need to be patched throughout a lifetime. Having the courage to explore your own cracks—your own areas of self-doubt and feelings of unworthiness—is deep, spiritual work. This work has much meaning as your cracks were made by past life experiences, which provides you now with the framework for self-growth.

Spirit lives inside you, even in the cracks. Although you may not see it, Spirit is there in all the crevices of your self-doubt and negative beliefs, as there is no part of you that Spirit rejects. Spirit is always there, offering you an alternative view if you are just quiet enough to hear it. Spirit sees you as you truly are, which is pure, brilliant light. As you begin to seal up your cracks with self-love, you will start to shine more brilliantly than ever before. You will start to radiate out the light from your own inner spirit. As this magnificent prism, you not only shine out your own inner brilliance, but you will also help others by reflecting their own light back onto themselves, allowing them to bathe in their own radiance. In this way, you can be a beacon to others, shining from within. Allowing others to see that you were once cracked and fragile, but are now strong and capable, embracing your true essence, which is divine love.

<u>Reflection Questions/Exercises:</u>

1. Are there any areas in your own life where you are noticing light escaping? Are there any areas of your life where you feel powerless, helpless, or not good enough?

2. For today, sit in a quiet, meditative state for 10-15 minutes. You may want to set a timer to go off at the allotted time, or you may choose to just do the meditation experience until it feels right for you to stop. To start, sit in a comfortable position and try to limit interruptions. Close your eyes and start to take slow, deep breaths. Focus on your breathing, inhaling and exhaling. Now, envision a healing green light in your heart. Feel this energy radiating in your core, warm and powerful. Sit with this warm, green light for as long as feels right to you and continue to inhale and exhale. When you are ready, begin to push this green, loving energy outward and feel this energy surround you. Enclose yourself in this green energy field and sit for the remaining time with this warm, loving energy circulating around you. During your meditation experience, if you find yourself getting distracted, focus back on your breathing until you feel centered again, and then continue with your exercise. If this visualization triggers any resistance or negative feelings from you, journal about those feelings after meditation and explore them further.

<u>Daily Mantra:</u>
   "My true essence is divine love."

Exercise 18: Overcoming Doubt
The Sound of Spirit

Self-doubt is a powerful deterrent to spiritual growth. For those that are analytical or skeptical, believing in concepts that cannot be rationally explained can be a challenge. Yet, with or without doubt, spiritual truths exist. The fact remains that you are a spiritual being living a physical life. Believe that there is something within you that is worth knowing. Your inner spirit was put in your body to be a powerful force in your life. If unimpeded, this love and guidance would fill you up and assist you until the end of your human existence. This knowing, this infinite wisdom, was not meant to be contained or lessened. Your inner spirit wants to come out and reveal itself to you.

However, when you block your own spirit by doubts and self-criticism, instead of this knowledge flowing through freely, it is boarded up and only available to come through as a trickle of insight—one small drop of guidance at a time. This drop can easily be missed in the loudness of your mind, which then creates further doubts and further barriers. Meanwhile, the analytical you is waiting for a roaring wave to come through to prove that your inner spirit is "real." Because you are not able to see Spirit in a large and tangible way, you continue to doubt yourself and further build up your wall of resistance.

Yet, this is the ultimate paradox. As long as you doubt yourself, you are blocking the majority of the energy from flowing. You wonder why Spirit does not come through stronger as you are waiting for a tidal wave—undeniable proof—before you will believe that Spirit is actually with you. You will never experience the tidal wave if you are too scared and skeptical to release the wall you have built inside yourself. You made it board by board by your own self-criticism, disbelief, doubt, and unworthy feelings. You further solidify this wall by looking outside of yourself for answers, and by entrusting others to provide you with your sense of self-worth.

Spirit lives inside of you. You are the only one that can "prove" anything to yourself. Validation is an inside job, but it requires you to be quiet with yourself in order to hear it. You must start to quiet the screaming, self-defeating, doubtful, and degrading voice inside of yourself in order to begin to hear the truth that is quietly waiting behind the wall. Spirit is truth and will appear once you give your permission for it to do so.

Set a new intention that you are going to have faith in yourself. This may take practice, but can be done. When you are faced with decisions, sit quietly and trust yourself to do what is right for you. Work on quieting your inner critic by rejecting negative thoughts and repeating to yourself the following mantra, "I trust myself, I trust Spirit."

Trusting yourself and living from a place of stillness is a process that takes time, but as you practice, you will start to open up your connection to your true self. Each time you have the courage to be authentic, to choose to love yourself, or to listen to your own intuition; you are breaking down the barrier. The more boards you remove inside, the more you will see Spirit working in your daily life. As your connection to Spirit grows, start to look for signs of this energy. How is your life being enhanced? The small things you notice can further cement to yourself the idea that Spirit is a real force, working tirelessly for you.

The irony is that once Spirit is allowed to show you its full grace and power unimpeded, you will be beyond the point of needing proof. Spirit will begin to be a seamless part of your life once you accept your own inner divineness. Give yourself this gift. Notice the small drips of Spirit that start to come through, they may be small and quiet at first but gain momentum with time. These drips turn into trickles, which turn into small streams, which then turn into rivers that will lead you directly to the ocean of your true self—infinite Spirit potential.

<u>Reflection Questions/Exercises:</u>

1. What are your beliefs about intuition? Do you believe that there is a part of you that is connected to Spirit? In what ways do you see Spirit working in your life already? In what ways would you like Spirit to come through stronger?

2. For today, sit in a quiet, meditative state for 10-15 minutes. You may want to set a timer to go off at the allotted time, or you may choose to just do the meditation experience until it feels right for you to stop. To start, sit in a comfortable position and try to limit interruptions. Close your eyes and start to take slow, deep breaths. Focus on your breathing, inhaling and exhaling. Now picture a white, brilliant light that is coming in from the top of your head, shining down to the bottom of your feet, like a cylinder. Situate yourself in your mind so you are sitting in this light, allowing it to shine straight through you. Imagine this is a beam of spiritual energy that is opening up your intuition and inner knowing. Continue to focus on your breathing, inhaling and exhaling, and sit in this warm light throughout the remainder of your meditation time, simply allowing it to flow through you. During your meditation experience, if you find yourself getting distracted, focus back on your breathing until you feel centered again, and then continue with your exercise. After the meditation, journal about any thoughts or emotions that came up for you. If any resistance to this exercise surfaced, explore that further as well.

<u>Daily Mantra:</u>

"I trust in Spirit to guide my life."

Exercise 19: Acceptance

Currents

Before your inner spirit came into the physical existence that you are currently experiencing, it set forth intentions and lessons that it wanted to learn in this lifetime. These intentions are powerful and have fueled and molded the life that you have lived up to this point. The challenges and trials that you have faced and will encounter stem from these intentions that were set forth upon you entering this life.

You may ask, "What exactly were my intentions?" A human mind does not enter life with the precise memory of what particular intentions you decided upon, as the mind would take this information and try to control all future outcomes, reducing the chance for spiritual advancement. Instead, intentions remain shrouded, working in the background, influencing your choices and interactions. There are a variety of ways that your life lessons can present themselves to you. Part of the spiritual growth process involves you encountering the lessons as they come up, one at a time, and being called upon to make changes day-by-day.

Without change, there would be little spiritual growth. Change can act as the catalyst to fuel a new way of life or to develop a different mindset. Without this catalyst, many people would continue on the same path indefinitely, as the human mind is one that likes consistency and predictability. It is a major life lesson to accept that change is not the enemy in life. Change is as essential for spiritual development as oxygen is for your physical body. Your spirit is excited for growth and change;

however, your mind often overrides that quest for growth by placing a layer of fear over all unknown outcomes.

Change can be painful at times. You may lose someone close to you and miss the physical life you shared together. Some part of your life may end—a relationship, a title, or a job. You may lose worldly possessions or suffer health problems that alter your self-perception. Being required to take a different course than you had originally planned can be challenging and seem burdensome at times. Being thrust into a different mindset can bring up many negative emotions, such as resentment, anger, or fear. You may have a knee-jerk reaction to push these negative feelings away; however, you must be able to experience these emotions before anything transformative can happen. Let yourself sit with these uncomfortable or painful experiences. You are strong enough to handle the feelings that come up, even if it feels that the emotional wave is going to crush you. It will not, as your inner spirit is indestructible and is being invigorated by this wave. Allow this current of emotion to carry you forward. Walk with the momentum that it provides. It is guiding you to new outcomes that are required for your inner spirit to progress and grow.

The contrasting choice is to resist and run from change, digging your heels into the ground and refusing to move with the current that is passing through your life. This feels even more crushing, as all your energy is being directed at resisting the current of change, instead of moving with it. You miss the lesson when your energy is tied up in a fear response of rejecting or trying to run from the oncoming wave. The waves are being created from your own intentions. They will continue to show up in your life in one way or another until you have successfully completed the lesson.

Having this knowledge can assist you on your path as it provides a context for the issues that come up in your life. Your life is not random chaos. Your life is not a mistake. You are living exactly the intentions you set forth in Spirit. You can start to get a sense of what your life's lessons are by reflecting back on the trials that you have already endured, and the problems that are coming up in your current life. What patterns are showing up over and over again? What are your painful areas of struggle?

Take time to sit quietly and begin to connect with your own inner spirit, which is a fountain of knowledge and guidance. Begin to live life from this place of inner quietness, which allows you to see your own struggles for what they really are—currents of change that bring opportunities for growth.

<u>Reflection Questions/Exercises:</u>

1. Review the difficult times you have had in your life. Are there any patterns or similarities that emerge? How have you dealt with these painful past experiences? Do you see any lessons that may be trying to come forward?

2. For today, if any difficult or negative emotions come up, notice what your knee-jerk reaction is. If you feel angry, do you start blaming others and project this anger outward? If someone makes a hurtful comment, do you think about it all day and get stuck rehearsing what you should or should not have said, trying to rationalize the event? Next, if you are able, after noticing the conditioned response that occurred inside of you, try instead to feel the negative emotion without having a judgment about it. Allow it to just be an emotion that you are temporarily experiencing and keep the energy moving. Instead of personalizing the experience and emotions that are coming up, label the emotion as a thing, such as the emotion called "anger" or "fear" and see this energy passing through you. Allow the energy to move along, instead of becoming stuck inside of you. Compare the difference in how this feels versus being weighed down with the experience for the rest of the day. Try experimenting with this in small ways first to gain practice, and then see if you can use this technique to clear some of the deeper-rooted hurts that live inside you. Again, allow yourself to feel the hurt and let it pass on, not running from it or condemning it. It may help to journal about the experiences as you clear them, to gain further clarity about them.

<u>Daily Mantra:</u>

"I see change for what it is, an opportunity for growth."

Exercise 20: Acceptance

Pebbles

Within you resides a piece of Spirit, which gives you the capacity to experience deep knowing and wisdom. This intuitive force that lives inside of you is a pool of light that radiates worthiness and love outward. It is all loving, all forgiving, casts no judgments, and gives every ounce of itself in order to support you. This pool is always available for you to tap into and to provide you with nourishment and essential hydration. If you are seeking guidance, quench your thirst for knowledge and truth from this internal pool, looking within to fill up your cup.

The individual path that you walk in this lifetime is connected to your inner pool of Spirit. This path is lined with pebbles, each one being a memory, a moment in your life that you have laid down beside you. Each pebble is a piece of your life that can never be changed, as time passes and cannot be reclaimed. Whether difficult or pleasant past experiences they may be, the pebbles are placed on the ground, one at a time, and slowly lead you to back to your golden pool. There is no need to go backward and pick up each piece, assessing if it was a good or bad pebble, as every past experience is an important part of your life and has led you to your current location. All pebbles eventually lead to the same destination, and each was chosen to be there for a reason. You cannot see it at the time that the pebbles are being placed, but when you look back down the path from a place of greater light, you can see each pebble fitting together perfectly for your feet to walk upon.

Your path may wind and get tricky to pass in places; however, there is always a light shining from within your pool of Spirit to guide you.

This light can be a beacon during challenging times and hope in the darkness if you remember to look for it. You are never truly lost, as your feet will always remain on your path, which is forever connected to Spirit. All lives eventually make it back to the water no matter how long or difficult the path may be.

Life moves on, and you will lay more pebbles down. You will step closer and closer to the radiant pool of Spirit until your feet reach the cool water. You will then know that the time is right, when your path is complete. Looking back in awe and wonder, you will be able to see your life for what it truly has been—a divine series of interwoven moments. A pebble masterpiece.

<u>Reflection Questions/Exercises:</u>

1. For today, sit in a quiet, meditative state for 10-15 minutes. You may want to set a timer to go off at the allotted time, or you may choose to just do the meditation experience until it feels right for you to stop. To start, sit in a comfortable position and try to limit interruptions. Close your eyes and start to take slow, deep breaths. Focus on your breathing, inhaling and exhaling. Now imagine that you are standing on your path and can see a pool of golden light in front of you. Notice the details, what does the scenery around you look like, how does the pool look to you? Take in your surroundings, then sit with this imagery and continue to gaze at your inner pool of knowing and just relax into this space for the length of your meditation experience. During your meditation experience, if you find yourself getting distracted, focus back on your breathing until you feel centered again, and then continue with your exercise.

2. After your meditation, journal about what feelings, thoughts, or emotions arose while you were sitting quietly in this internal place. Follow whatever thread you start journaling about and continue to write until it feels appropriate to stop.

<u>Daily Mantra:</u>

"My life is a pebble masterpiece."

Exercise 21: Worthiness

Wide Open Doors

The journey of feeling worthy and of loving yourself can feel like a never-ending climb up a steep and rocky mountain. Every time you feel you have the right footing, just the right momentum going, the rocks can shift, and you find yourself falling and grasping for something to hold on to. Searching for a lifeline, trying to remember why it was that you loved yourself, and coming up empty handed. Many feel that they have fallen off the mountain of worthiness so many times, that getting to the top would be an insurmountable task. Perhaps you believe that you are somehow so broken, unlovable, and flawed that you are not even worthy of the possibility of starting the climb. So, you stay on the ground and remain in a state of self-hatred, doubt, and fear.

Many people are so used to living in the cold shadow of this giant mountain that they forget that there is even a mountain of worthiness there. All they see is a giant black mass—darkness that fills up their daily life to the point that they almost forget what color looks like—as their eyes are always looking down. This is the life of many people on the planet today, but it is not the natural state that a person is supposed to be. Every person comes to this life with an inner spirit, a connection to the greater Spirit, which is pure love. You enter this life being worthy, just because you are alive.

Return to the mountain of worthiness and see it with your true eyes, which are the eyes of your inner spirit. If you are able to do this, you will see the reality of the situation. There actually is no enormous mountain that you have to climb to feel worthy. There is no special gear to buy, as you are not going on a mountaineering adventure. The truth is that you are standing on your path of worthiness already. Once this truth starts to come back to you, you will see that you are holding a flashlight. Turn on the flashlight and look straight ahead of you, not up. There is a door in this mountain. It was so dark with your eyes downward cast that you did not see that this door was open the entire time, wide open. Step inside the door and feel the warmth inside. You are now standing inside worthiness. Notice that you have not gained any elevation. You have not struggled, climbing up a steep cliff. You literally just opened your eyes, took a step, and now are in warmth and light instead of freezing darkness. This is the first step, awakening to your potential. Realizing that this possibility is open to you, just as it is open to everyone. Stepping into the light makes it is easier to remember your truth. You always knew this place existed inside the mountain, but you had somehow forgotten about it along the way. You are protected and warm here in this place and are safe.

Your fear voice may be trying to object at this point, stating that you do not belong in this space. Fear may be trying to remind you of all the times that you made a wrong choice, reminding you of all the reasons why "someone like you" does not deserve to feel worthy. Now is the time to erase this voice from your existence. Leave this voice outside in the cold darkness. Remember this: worthiness is not bought by perfection in this lifetime. All human lives have missteps along the way. Your life is more than a collection of your worst mistakes. You are still worthy no matter what choices you have made in the past. Big or small mistakes, every person is worthy.

Accept that you belong in the security of the mountain of worthiness because you are alive. Spirit is with you and wants you to be warm and loved. Step inside and shut the door, leave the cold behind. Start to live from this place and explore the safety of realizing that you are wanted in this life, you are needed in this life. It may take a while for this to sink in. You can stay protected in the mountain for as long as it takes you to fully remember and accept your innate essentialness.

Once your sense of worthiness kicks in fully, notice that there is another door straight ahead of you, and you are free to walk through it and explore what life has to offer, it is a vast world of potential. You will notice that you are no longer cold as you are now being warmed from within. Spirit is warming you with an inner sun that shines brightly forever, and you can now move forward confidently. There may be obstacles up ahead that you will encounter, but nothing is insurmountable when you trust yourself, and trust in Spirit. Lastly, remember that you are a beautiful and divine being, you are worthy in every way, Spirit loves you dearly, and you are free.

<u>Reflection Questions/Exercises:</u>

1. For today, sit in a quiet, meditative state for 10-15 minutes. You may want to set a timer to go off at the allotted time, or you may choose to just do the meditation experience until it feels right for you to stop. To start, sit in a comfortable position and try to limit interruptions. Close your eyes and start to take slow, deep breaths. Focus on your breathing, inhaling and exhaling. Envision yourself in the mountain of worthiness as previously described. Feel the warmth and safety of being in this place of light, and sit with this feeling of security and love during your meditation. If any fear thoughts come in that are distracting or trying to interject, imagine shutting the door to this negativity and return again to the feeling of warmth and light. Take in the details surrounding you and bask in the love and light that this safe refuge provides. During your meditation experience, if you find yourself getting distracted, focus back on your breathing until you feel centered again, and then continue with your exercise.

2. Journal immediately after the above exercise about any feelings or thoughts that came up during meditation regarding worthiness. Ask for guidance from your own inner spirit about any issues that you need further clarity about or that would be helpful for you to explore, such as ongoing perceptions that you hold that you are somehow unlovable or not good enough. Follow whatever thread you start journaling about and continue to write until you feel you have reached a stopping point.

<u>Daily Mantra:</u>

"I am worthy simply because I am alive."

NOTES

NOTES

75

NOTES

NOTES

NOTES

NOTES

79

NOTES

NOTES

81

NOTES

NOTES

NOTES

NOTES

85

NOTES

NOTES

87

NOTES

NOTES

89

NOTES

NOTES

NOTES

NOTES

93

NOTES

Acknowledgements

To my wonderful husband Brandon, for being a constant source of support, love and security. I am so blessed to have you in my life and I appreciate everything you have done for me. I love you babe!

To Jameson, for reminding me of my capacity to love unconditionally. You are truly a gift from Spirit and I cherish every moment we spend together.

To Heather, for being a beacon of light on this spiritual journey. Thank you for encouraging me and giving me the support I needed at each stage of this process. This book would not exist without you!

To Heidi, for being a guide and mentor on my spiritual journey. Thank you for believing in me and reminding me that I am a spiritual being. You have truly changed my life and I am so grateful to you.

To my friends and family, thank you for providing me with the life experiences that have led me down my path. I appreciate all your love and support.

To Janet Devlin, for editing this book with skill and love.

About the Author

Stephanie Clark is a psychiatric/mental health nurse practitioner living in Idaho. She is passionate about helping others live an empowered existence and has worked in the mental health field for ten years. She enjoys spending time with her family, traveling and exploring the beauty that life has to offer.

Connect with Stephanie Clark:
https://www.facebook.com/SClarkInspirations/
Stephanie Clark (@S_Clark186) | Twitter
https://www.smashwords.com/profile/view/StephanieClark

Inspirations

Made in the USA
Monee, IL
07 July 2026

56552421R00059